Emotionally Bankrupt

Don't ever lose
your spark.

Stay shining,

Jenny

Emotionally Bankrupt

Jennifer Martin

Emotionally Bankrupt

Copyright © 2019 by Jennifer Martin. All rights reserved.

Contents

Dedication

To my parents, as all they ever wanted
was for me to be happy.

Mom and Dad, writing makes me happy.

Acknowledgements

To Celeste Ellis. You were the first to read my poetry and encourage I share it with the world (*all 1,000 of my Instagram followers*). You will forever push me in yoga, in philosophy, and in believing in myself.

To Amy Hulse. My life coach, my cheerleader. Thank you for listening to every last rant and reading every new material. Without your insight I would still be in an office, crying in bathroom stalls between sales calls.

To Rick Stasi. The person "who would change my life". The butterfly effect that sparked hope into my artistic direction. You opened up doors and ideas I could have never dreamed up on my own.

To every friend that sat through open mic night as I waited for my turn on stage. To every friend that showed up to my first show amidst a snow storm. To the refined young ladies and gentlemen who have been with me since day one. Without your encouragement, this book would have gone unseen to the public. You believed in me more than I could ever have on my own.

Thank you for reading every poem I texted your way.
Thank you for supporting me when
I wanted to quit my job.
Thank you for supporting me when I quit my job.

Thank you for teaching me how to date
&
Thank you for the love you showed me
when I wasn't loving myself.

It is through your motivation in which I
grew the strength to share this story.

Prologue

Like many privileged millennials, I was raised *knowing* I was special. Growing up with continuous praise over my significance drove me to become a confident teenager and a talented athlete. I didn't run around with the cool kids, but I had a lot of friends. And while I knew I was special, talented and loved, I was fearful that my shiny uniqueness would soon wear off.

This worry was easily suppressed when I started college. Not from the alcohol, but from the rush of independence and attention I received freshman year. Though after I learned how to balance sports practices, class, and dating my first boyfriend, an obsession to fine-tune my perfectionism began to bud. I had flirted with anorexia at the end of high school and by sophomore year at university, my "lean" meals escalated to nibbling carrots for dinner. I was put on an eating plan and required to visit the school psychologist between weekly weigh-ins. This disease nearly cost me my athletic career before I ended it on my own to enjoy my senior year as a "regular" student, and opted to study abroad.

During my semester in Italy I began eating carbs for the first time in years. Those carbs led to more carbs which led to my first bout of bulimia. I did not start gelato-hopping until that last month abroad, in which I gained 22 pounds in the course of three weeks. It was during that stretch of time and pant size that the reality of going home took hold of me. I would soon trade my foreign adventures for the mundane job that awaited me after graduation.

And so I said to hell with it.

I continued travelling, packing my eating disorder with me. While I knew I needed help, I was determined to chase a life full of diverse, cultural experiences which led me to sell artwork on cruise ships. While my position was tasteful, the way I behaved around the buffet was not. An intense fear of clogging the ship's septic system after a purge triggered a half-hour panic attack in my cabin the day of my resignation. This chapter of ship-life was over, but my passion to travel prevailed. I then migrated to a country whose cuisine was one of which I could not possibly binge on: South Korea.

Another year of liked Instagram photos and stamps in my passport accompanied another year of bingeing, but not necessarily purging. By this time, I was tired. I was tired of the chase to be thin. I was tired of spending money on trips I couldn't afford. I was tired of introducing myself to international friends because by this time, I wasn't sure who I was.

By spring of 2017, I returned to my parents' house with an expanded waistline and an empty wallet. I had convinced myself that maybe it was time to conform. To start facing adulthood and stop chasing special. And with the guidance of my peers, I landed a 9-5 and downloaded dating apps.

For a year, I worked for the man in a corporate office while working to land a man from my phone. The more emails I sent and profiles I swiped, the more I felt confused and exhausted. I thought that keeping a steady job and gaining male attention would fix my funk with eating and bring purpose to my life. And while I made much progress with my eating disorder through rest and recovery, I soon realized that living with an eating disorder has nothing to do with food, but with the way I react to my feelings.

For a year, I started writing down these feelings in a form of poetry that is authentically me. Instead of eating over a bad day at work, I wrote about it. Instead of eating over a boy, I wrote about him. And I am still writing despite quitting my job and deleting the apps.

My soul has been sucked.

My heart has been broken.

My poetry is all I have left to give to the world as I have become Emotionally Bankrupt.

WERK

I sat crying in my manager's office:
"I just can't do this anymore"

Foreword

The artist in me would rather starve
Than stare at the screen which feeds me

Interviews

Tell me about yourself
Not who you are, but why I should like you
Describe a time when you succeeded
If the answer is impressive, I don't care if it's true
Tell me your strengths
Things you think you're good at and how it relates
What are your weaknesses?
You admit you have weaknesses?
If given the opportunity, what will you do?
What else can you prove?
Why do you want the job?
Why you?

First Day

Everyone is nice
Everyone is smiling
Everyone shakes my hand before they start dialing

In the break room somebody asks me my name
They tell me this job is more so a game
A game about numbers, a game about people
This job is a competition, but we are all treated equal

Everyone is nice
Everyone buys my lunch
They give me advice to soak up like a sponge

In the bathroom somebody asks how I'm doing
I say "just fine" as I wash my hands with soap
They tell me to "fake it 'til I make it"
I say I'm good at faking it, but they didn't get the joke

Everyone is nice
Everyone is fine
Everything is great, it's just a matter of time

Meetings

Making goals of making goals
To feel like we are winning
Setting meetings about meetings
To talk about our goals
All this talk
All these meetings
All the emails in between
Never understanding my true role
Beyond service to the queen

The Bobs

Handshakes as stiff as their smiles
Make ways down the line
"Hi, I'm Bob, nice to meet you"
"I'm here to waste your time"
Bob's been here for 30 years
Bob knows what's up
He'll offer you the Kool-aid
But won't let you drink from his cup

K-Cups

I run on gasoline
Black and bitter
Fueling my morning so I can GO GO GO

I pump my gasoline
From an industrial Keurig
Waiting in line and saying "HELLO"

I drink the gasoline
Though it's not premium
For its all I have and all that I know

My Bad

I
will
not
apologize
for
the mistake
I made
on
Monday

Morning Affirmations

"I like my job"
"I like my job"
"I like my job"
"I like my job"
"I like my job"
"I like my job"
"I like my job"
"I like my job"
"I like my job"
"I like my job"
"I like my job"
"I like my job"
"I like my job"
"I like my job"
"I like my job"
"I like my job"
"I like my job"
"I like my job"
"I like my job"
"I like my job"
"I like my job"
"I like my job"
"I like my job"
"I like my job"
"I like my job"
"I like my job"
"I like my job"
Is what I say to myself in the mirror

I Never Used to Have a Fear of Flying

I am set to autopilot
From the hours of 9 to 5
Circling above the runway
Desperately awaiting
My descend home

Bots

I feel a beat inside of me
I know how to love and care
But when I check my reflection
All I see is a robot with hair

PTO

We wouldn't need sick days
If our job provided life

Zombies

Call me a daydreamer
But never will you see me
Sleepwalking through the day

The Hive

Hurdled in harmony
Between cups of caffeine
The bees and phones start buzzing
Some bees fly by
Some serve the queen
And some pretend to be humming
To pick up the pace
They analyze flow
Of who's chasing nectar
And who'll be let go

RISE AND GRIND RISE AND GRIND RISE AND
GRIND RISE AND GRIND RISE AND GRIND
RISE AND GRIND RISE AND GRIND RISE AND
GRIND RISE AND GRIND RISE AND GRIND
RISE AND GRIND RISE AND GRIND RISE AND
GRIND RISE AND GRIND RISE AND GRIND
RISE AND GRIND RISE AND GRIND RISE AND
GRIND RISE AND GRIND RISE AND GRIND
RISE AND GRIND RISE AND GRIND RISE AND
GRIND RISE AND GRIND RISE AND GRIND
RISE AND GRIND RISE AND GRIND RISE AND
GRIND RISE AND GRIND RISE AND GRIND
RISE AND GRIND RISE AND GRIND RISE AND
GRIND RISE AND GRIND RISE AND GRIND
RISE AND GRIND RISE AND GRIND RISE AND
GRIND RISE AND GRIND RISE AND GRIND
RISE AND GRIND RISE AND GRIND RISE AND
GRIND RISE AND GRIND RISE AND GRIND
RISE AND GRIND RISE AND GRIND RISE AND
GRIND RISE AND GRIND RISE AND GRIND
RISE AND GRIND RISE AND GRIND RISE AND
GRIND RISE AND GRIND RISE AND GRIND
RISE AND GRIND RISE AND GRIND RISE AND
GRIND RISE AND GRIND RISE AND GRIND
RISE AND GRIND RISE AND GRIND RISE AND
GRIND RISE AND GRIND RISE AND GRIND RISE
AND GRIND RISE AND GRIND RISE AND GRIND
RISE AND GRIND RISE AND GRIND RISE AND
GRIND RISE AND GRIND RISE AND GRIND
RISE AND GRIND RISE AND GRIND **RISE**.

Posters

Company values plastered in view
But does this company value me?
Signs of smiling faces
'Bout honor, service,
And integrity
A model of financial health
Beacons of hope
Of promise and wealth
Joy slapped across these figurines
Someone was paid for such a thing
To pose for a poster
To be put on display
On a corporate office wall
To lighten a worker's workday
But who am I to say
I keep pictures of a better place
Bullited upon my work space
Something pulled from a magazine
So my eyes can drift into another scene
The internet's no good,
I'd rather daydream
Save web browsing for later
It's a digital world
Yet it's all about the paper

Confession

I faked a funeral
When a part of me started dying

I Took That Day Off To Write

The longer I stare at this blank screen
The larger my anxiety builds
As the irony of writing
Is that when we have the time and place
We cannot seem to find the headspace

Latters

They told me
To be a go-getter
But I had loved what I'd got
They told me
That work will bring purpose
As long as you climb to the top
They told me
They daily grind
Will pay for a home
I told them
I pride myself
In finding comfort
Outside my comfort zone

Resentment

This bean water is a sad excuse for coffee
It is jet fuel that does not help me propel
My computer is a poor man's Macbook
Crashing down when I open Excel
These fluorescent lights do not show me the way
These folder cabinets are not going to save me
My paychecks don't show my worth
And this work cannot be defining

Take a Deep Breath

On the days you woke up on Tuesday
Thinking it was Friday
On the mornings you spilled coffee
And hit every red light
During those lunches you ate at your desk
To keep up with demands
For the nights you stayed late
To hit your quota
Remember that you are more than a title
And you can always go home
Turn your day back around
And unwind.

Be grateful
For this is just a job
It is a means to an end
It is just a job
It is never the end

Labor of Love

My love, unlike a job,
Is irreplaceable
I will never climb the ladder
For a title
I will not use apps
To passively look for new opportunities
I will not take time off
I will not take sick days
But my love,
Like my job,
Requires devotion
And will never stop working

Hiding

How humiliating it is
To have my bare bottom sink into a porcelain pot
While I muffle my cry
Mustering peace between the stall

How odd it might be
If someone found me
More in tune with myself
Here
Alone in this bathroom
Than producing behind a desk

How obvious is it
That I was alone in the bathroom
Hiding
From producing behind my desk

Letter of Resignation

It not you, it's me
It's a little bit of everything
This place. This scene.
Is not what I expected it to be

I thought I would be happy
Sitting behind a screen
I thought I would feel normal
In an office working

I thought a 9 to 5
Was a part of the American Dream
But a woman with a wild heart
Can't keep a white collar clean

What was I thinking?
I would be saved by stability?
No steady paycheck
Can write off my dignity

And I do not mean
To condescend my colleagues
They are lovely people
We just think differently

They got the hang of things
As I cried quietly
Hovering under the radar
Everyday, fighting

Some people are born for this work
To lead and support their family
I was born to write words
Now these words will set me free

Thank you for your time
For this opportunity
But I must finish my job
Of becoming the person
I was meant to be

Promises

They told me pencil skirts
Would write my success story

THE VOICE
INSIDE MY HEAD

There is no cure
There is only hope

Serenity Prayer

God,

Grant me the serenity

To accept the things I cannot change

The courage to change the things I can

& The wisdom to know the difference

Addict

Everyone is addicted to their phones
I mean
You're on yours right now[†]
Some people are alcoholics
The rest are just functioning
There are those that steal
That stream porn
And hoard
But me?
My addiction isn't cool
It's not one often highlighted in movies
Or disguised in a club
My addiction is ugly. It's counterproductive. It's well, borderline accepted in our society
You ate too much?
Throw it up
You had a second serving?
Skip lunch tomorrow
Did you really not substitute a salad for fries?
Looks like you're working out twice today
My addiction is one which I cannot abstain from the source
You have a problem with alcohol?
Stop. Drinking.
You shoot up to take away the pain?

[†] This poem was written on a phone, shared on a phone, and originally read on stage from a phone

Stop. Using.
So simple, right?
If only my issue could be taken away
by taking away the food
But I already tried that
60 pounds ago
I restricted, I binged, I purged
And now I am nothing but a body
waiting for it's next meal
I am an addict, alight
But not the cool type

Anorexia

I want to disappear

Brain Food

I should be reading textbooks
Instead of nutrition labels
I should be writing my thesis
Not this tragic fable

Each story the same
It always begins with "why?"
"Why hasn't the scale moved down?"
"All I've done is try!"

I should be thinking about tests
Instead of thinking about food
I should be in the library
But I'm eating in the nude

Each bite that I take
Is counted and recorded
Each calorie consumed
Is burned or aborted

I should be studying
I should be in class
But my mind is so tired
And deprived from this fast

Artificial Sweetener

Your lips
Became my latest diet
I cut the sweet out of my life
And restricted myself to you
Funny how something sugar free
Could taste so good to me
Malnourishment led to misbehaving
Lashing out when I couldn't fix my craving
Your lips
Led me to lose weight
I wanted to be yours
So I never ate

Gasoline

They say food is fuel
Just like gasoline
And so I fill up my tank

But there's premium and diesel and unleaded to choose
from
So I pick from the bottom of the rank

"You're using unleaded!"
"Why'd you do that?"
"You're going to crash"
"Or worse, get fat"

"Did I say fat?"
"I meant get a flat"

"You'll lose control of the wheel and fall off track"

Because food is fuel
And if it's not exact
We run out of power
And that is a fact

Reflections

I didn't starve myself to disappear
But to be noticed
I thought being small
Meant being wanted

I didn't starve myself for the fear of being large
But out of fear of being average
I wanted them to point and say
"She's got it"

I starved myself
Not because I was deprived
But because I wasn't enough
At least, that's what I told myself

I starved myself
Out of attention
Out of worry and rebellion

Because if I could control what goes in
I could predict what went out
At least, that's what I told myself

Bulimia

Make it go away

Willpower

My hands are not connected to my head
When I tell myself to put it down
"You don't need that" I'll say
But soon I put the food in my mouth
"You're not hungry, so why must you eat?"
I look at my hands
With a sense of defeat
I put my hands on my head
To decide if I'll put my fingers in my mouth
My hands aren't connected to my head
Now my hands are empty
And my head is filled with doubt

Yo-Yo

I've gained and lost weight
Always careful to hide it
My closet is filled
With a full scale of sizes
My scale shows a number
I'm too afraid to read
Because when I do
There are never sweet surprises

I diet, I indulge
I count each calorie
Whenever I eat too much
My finger is my remedy
I try and I try
To fight my obsession
So I go to meetings
And make a confession

But what I admit aloud
Won't change what I do alone
I say I want to be healthy
But my disease wants me
Thin to the bone

Take the Compliment

They tell me I'm a pretty girl but
There's nothing pretty about what I do
"You have a beautiful smile" they say
Without knowing what this smile's been through
Men have quoted me as "sexy"
But would they still say that if they knew?
All the glutinous, ugly things
This pretty girl's been up to

Envy

I want to look like her
And she wants to look like me
I want my collarbone to show
She wants my Double D's

Some want longer hair
Or a gap between the knees
Some long for six packs
And whiter, straighter teeth

But I want to look like her
The one in the magazine
Instead I look in the mirror
And my head starts to scream

"Your lips look fine"
"Your eyeliner, too"
"But your cheeks are bloated"
"From that thing that you do"

I wash off my face
And start to undress
I brush my teeth
And take a deep breath

You don't look like her
You don't have to
God made us all beautiful
And that includes you

Binging

Not enough

Target

Everyone is out to get me
Starting with my jeans
They are fighting my thighs
As I get in between

You don't deserve me anymore!
They scream
Go back to the gym
Go back to eighteen
Go back to the time when your spine could be seen
Go back
Go back
And for God's sake, eat clean

Everyone is out to get me
Including my fridge
When I open it up
It turns on my switch

You are kidding yourself!
Mocking me like a bitch
Demanding certain foods, but I can't tell which
Eat the fruit
Eat the spinach
Eat everything and watch it vanish

Everyone is out to get me
Telling me what to do
Everyone is judging
Watching my every move

Can everyone please
Calm the f*** down!
I am trying
I am trying
I am trying
To drown out the sounds

EAT CAKE

The rich stay skinny
Ordering food to waste
They take pictures of their meals
Only for a taste

No to-go boxes
No dessert
Unless it's for Insta
Then a bite wouldn't hurt

Chew slowly
And then spit it out
You can afford the world
But you can't afford to burn out

Take it all
Take it all in
Over consuming
While remaining thin

The rich stay skinny
Because beauty is power
So if the money runs out
They can still run and devour

Purge

On my knees for neither him nor Him

Balance

I know what's best for me. I know what to eat. I know kale is a better source of calcium than milk and there is more fiber in chickpeas than there are in those synthetic granola bars. I know too much sugar will make my chin break out and my stomach soft. I know that when I don't eat my vegetables, I get lethargic and fall into a binge of caffeine and carbs. I know that this diet isn't sustainable but it's all I look forward to when I wake up in the morning after a night of dreaming. Dreams of the skinny body I once had are disturbed by a nightmare of reality. Mirrors and scales haunt my thoughts when I wake up so I drown myself in sleep aids and alcohol to escape into my dreams again.

I know what's best for me.

I know that if I burn more calories than I consume, I have a chance of being skinny again. I know that this formula takes time but I am lost for time. I am tired of waiting. I know that I must be patient with my body. Allow it to heal and allow it to rest. But in between the rest and the sleep and the dreaming I must work to remove all which I have gained. All that weighs me down.

I know what's best for me.

I realize that every morning is an opportunity to hit refresh and forgive myself for the damage I caused the day before. But every morning the mirror and the scale remind me that I am far from my dreams. I am far from being skinny.

But I know what's best for me.

And I'll continue to force salad on my plate when all I want is cheese and I'll go on a walk instead of smoking weed. Or maybe I'll do a little bit of both because this life is about balance and when you stop needing the scale, you find intuition.

I know what's best for me.

And that's a start.

Reunions

College educated but I'm still insane
I study others, learning how to behave
I follow their lead
I see what they eat
Someone takes a cracker
And I feel relieved
So I take a cracker
And I take some cheese
Chewing slowly I smile
Washing it away
With Pinot Gris

Communications major but I'm lost with words
When they ask me how I'm doing
I say "fine" and observe
They all look fine
They all look thin
They all think I'm fine
But they don't know where I've been
I've been hiding away between
Cookies and cakes
I was out eating
While they were on dates
Dates turned to partners
My only dates are dried fruit
Now they fight with their partners
All I fight with is food

But partners forgive
And partners support
I try being my own partner
But I always fall short

A popular girl but I still feel alone
I slap myself sober
And starting heading home
I say goodbye to my lovers and friends
I say to myself
"You did good tonight"
"So avoid the drive thru and just go to bed"

A Letter to my Stomach

How are you so good to me? After years of taking abuse. How are you so resilient from each violent episode I've thrown your way?

You don't deserve it.
The abuse.
You never deserve it.

I want to apologize for every ice cream cone I've forced on you and demanded back. Or the meals I've refused because I wanted to make you small. I want to apologize for the meals I ate after I ate. You must have been so confused. You only tried to warn me with moans and signals to my head. But I don't listen. I never listen.

I want to listen and some days I do, but please know that you aren't the only one delivering messages about the food. There is something else. Or someone. Sometimes the voice sounds like me and sometimes it goes away. I try so hard to muffle this voice and I pray for it to stop. I pray! And I never pray.

I pray for this voice and I pray for my health and I pray for you. I pray for you as I am forever grateful for you. Even though I've hated you when you were thin and I've hated you when you were fat. And all you've done is try to love and nourish me back.

You didn't deserve it.
The hate.
You haven't done anything to deserve it.

So please, please accept this letter as a token of grace. A declaration of peace. A commitment to pray in helping this voice go away. You never give up on me, and I am ready to stop giving up on you.

Thank you.

Thank you.

Sincerely,

Jenny

Alternative Vices

Drinking to get drunk
To forget, to have fun
Smoking to relieve
A day that is done

Eating to fill
An emptiness inside
Netflix and Chilling
Netflix and hide

Swiping and liking
Checking who's seen
A story you created
Of reality's dream

What does it look like
To be sober
To be clean

How does it feel
To create, to be
What does it look like
To put something out there that is me

Instead of consuming
Well darling,
It feels free

Everything Causes Cancer

Healthy is happy
But we live in a world of drugs, pollution and gluten
Saying yes to everything
Forgetting the power of no

Healthy is happy
But what about bread
The essence of existence
The original offering
Bread is the body of life
But now bread is marked as bad
We would rather eat the flesh of an animal
Than the God-forbidden grain

Healthy is happy
But what about travel
The motive to immerse
Is now owned by Guy Fieri
Boarding planes for photo ops
Cruising the Caribbean
Between buffets and drink packages
Buying blood diamonds
And anything but local

Healthy is happy
But what about drugs
Ecstasy is in the name
30 minutes of bliss
Depending on your budget
But what about bars
What about clubs
Dancing until two
Puking until Monday

Fun does not sustain
Joy cannot be bought
Happy is healthy
And health is much simpler than we thought

Hope

There is hope in the moments between meals
Where I focus on You, and not the food
Those little moments when I am at peace
I can then express gratitude
Because when I put my hands in prayer
They are filled with hope
And not food
Hope is everything in my recovery
And hope begins with You

Everything is a Trigger

I want to be healthy
So I go to Whole Foods
Stock up on kombucha
Buy all the produce
I then remember that I am trying to save
And so I am triggered,
go home and misbehave

I want to be strong
So I go to Yoga Sculpt
I see impeccable bodies
And expect the same result
But when I go home and I take off my clothes
I am triggered by a reflection
My body doesn't come close

I want to be loved
So I go on dates
With men I have vetted
Who are cute and relate
I listen and laugh and I offer my body
I am triggered when I realize
All I can offer is my body

I want to be normal
So I picked a normal job
I hated that job
Now this book's all I got
I left that job when I was triggered by fear
Of not living to tell this story
But now the book is real
It is here

Everything is a trigger
But I am bulletproof

SCRAPS

Of Men and Messages

PART I

He said I was intense
As if love is mild

C'mon, Love a Little

Death and heartbreak are both for certain
That is, unless,
You choose to neither live nor love

Ambitions

Pursuing you
And all that you do
Wishfully thinking
All my dreams will come true

Maybe you'll ask
For me to be yours
Maybe one day
You'll arrive at my door

With flowers and wine
And a kiss to my forehead
You'll ask if I
Will be your girlfriend

I chased you over my dreams

Initial Feelings

I don't like the virtual you
The reply-after-an-hour you
I don't like the way you text
Or don't
I can't understand why you call
No one ever calls anymore
But you do
I don't like how you invite me over
To hang out with your friends
Because it makes me wonder
Am I just your friend?
I don't like the way you make me wait to kiss you
But I like you
I like you

Schooled

I was never crazy
About math and science
Every question
Only had one answer
Then I learned
In English lit
That there are a million ways
To say I love you

Time Will Tell

We are all given 24 hours in a day
But what we have is timeless
No need to wear a watch
When my eyes are set on you
We'll let the sunrise tell time
Manipulating minutes
To spend on each other

Patience

Study their eyes
Study their hands
Study their actions
Without making demands
Simply observe
Without saying a word
Just let them be
And maybe
Just maybe
They will be ready
To teach you something

Opposites Attract

You wanted to take my breath away
But I wanted to cry out your name

Tango

Dancing with you
Like the smoke off a flame
Intrepid and uninterrupted
Let's move through the night
Fueled by candlelight
Tend to our fire
And never neglect it

Bruises

I held out my hands
To show you the scars
I caught when I fell for you
You kissed them so softly
But never thought to ask
If I suffered
From internal bleeding

Sanity

I will lose my mind
Before I lose you
And so I become aloof
To avoid becoming alone

Crash

I felt it coming
And in a blink
Your head on collision
Left me in derbies

The Talk

I'm afraid to ask what you're afraid to say
So instead we sit in silence
The lights go out but I didn't flip the switch
And I reach for your hand in guidance
I yell all hell
Accusing you for this blackout
But you didn't respond
You didn't even shout
The lights came back on
The blame was acquitted
You may be responsible
But you'll never be committed

Glimpse

When everything is temporary
We made time stand still
The night grew on
But our spark remained
In those moments we were in bliss
Indifferent to the world
We took a taste
The aroma faded
The sun rose
We said goodbye
Everything is temporary

Long Distance

I was a wanderer
And I never stayed long
Chasing down the rush of a first day
Of new sights, heights and feels
Falling in love with foreign faces

I was a traveler
Moving along from home to home
But I could never seem
To check out with you

The First Poem I Wrote On A Typewriter

You captured time
To distract me from the tide
You locked me in your eyes
Anchoring down
So when I blinked up
I saw you
From underwater

Queen of Hearts

If you play your cards right,
You might just trick them into loving you

Swimming

I wanted to swim through time
As if we had an ocean to cross
Pacing steadily but you
Only knew
How to sprint

Just Say No

D.A.R.E. told me
LSD scooped your brain like ice cream
I learned on my own that
ILY had the same effect on the heart

Those three words
Are acid to my ears

I listened.

I've dabbled in the past
But when I tripped on you
Something about me
Will never be the same again

Writer's Block

I want to write about love stories
Like the songs we hear on the radio
Instead I write about you
After all, we only write what we know

Haiku #1

I never did say
Anything foul about you
I kissed and smiled

Hiding behind teeth
Were examples of contempt
Acutely swallowed

Fake Love

If it's too hard to say
Or you feel ashamed to scream it aloud
It's not love

Gateway

Like a drug
You were hard to come by
Meeting incognito, I played cool

Like a drug I was told to stay away
No one told me about *this* high
I was taught to avoid abuse

Like a drug
I inhaled
Lost inhibition
Evaded reality

But like a drug
You ran out
And I came down
Back to solitude and sanity

Fuego

When did we decide to put
Love
On the backburner?
Turning to Tinder
To spark a connection
You can stay home
With your safe electricity
I'm headed out
To start a forest fire

Songs With The Curse Words

Each party has an after party
That dries up from the sun
Everybody has a lover
Until everybody's gone

Everyone has a drink
Something to take in
But you and I have something here
So stay here
Stay here

Each song begins
With a beat drop
Each song has an encore
Which makes that beat drop

Every rapper speaks in curse words
Every song about drugs
Sex
& Rape
Every song with the curse words
Make me beat, bump, shake

These songs with the curse words
They sound so wrong
But this drink feels good
So I'll just sing along

Everyone has a drink
Something to take in
But you and I have something here
So don't leave
Stay here
Stay here

Ashes

He said it in his eyes
I caught him burning a fire
Without creating any light

It Starts With a Snap

Mind becoming mush
As hearts melt away
Two eyes hunger
Ears dissipate
Why listen when we breathe
In images from a screen
Why talk it out when we can numb
Sensory feelings
They say sadness cuts open wounds
To feel a better pain
I say sadness lifts it's finger
Only to hit pause and play
Sadness uses that same finger
To scroll throughout the day
Consuming the lives of others
Because we know no other way
Remember when we talked without phones
When we laughed without being recorded?
Remember how we waited for photos
To develop without being forwarded?
Remember when date night
Just meant you and me
Now I share you with the world
And the world is all following

I don't want to see you anymore
Because I see you through a screen
My mind is becoming mush
And my heart,
My heart is still melting

Low-Sodium Diet

Something about you
Tasted funny
So I took you in with a grain of salt
And overtime
Suffered from heart disease

Pick Up Lines

Don't call her beautiful until you get to know her

Fall

You were the first cool breeze
To end a hot summer
I sipped on your refreshments
Like cold water
Where were you
In June?
And where will you be
When there are no leaves on the trees?
I realize this chill will not last forever
Now your cool breeze
Feels awfully bitter

Anxieties

I imagined a world without you
Until it became my reality

Visa Required

I travel the world
Revisiting cities I have once loved
But no plane ticket
Will bring me back to you

Done

You are all the books I started
But never read through the ending
The nightmare I wake up from right before I die
You are all the love songs I cannot finish
Because you left without saying goodbye

Ghost

You wanted me to have the last word
And so you never replied

Sober

I don't get high anymore
Not like I used to
It triggers painful memories
Of crashing down with you

False Perceptions

You are not
Who I wanted
You to be

Mindfulness

Weakness became her biggest worry
She soon believed she wasn't worthy
How small and alone this girl must feel
Thinking he used her for a thrill
She removed herself from the world of him
Embracing the now, forgetting the then
She receded to her original wavelength
And observed the power of her own strength

Finite

You are now a memory
That too shall fade away

Jealous

I am so fortunate that
Envy is not a sensation I endure
When it comes to the lifestyles of others
I don't wish for that house
Or that car
Or those clothes
But when it comes to love
I will see a couple smiling
And be paralyzed in fear
That what they have
Is what I lost
And everything I crave to have again

Uninvited

Leave your shoes at the door before you walk all over me

Homophones

You took a piece of my heart
For your own peace of mind
Filling a void
Avoiding loneliness
You said no to devotion
Didn't know why I got mad
But said 'I love you' anyway
You said 'I love you' anyway
I lied in your bed
You lied when you said
That I was special to you
Making me believe I was special to you
A few weeks went by
You never said goodbye
So I spent my days
Kept in a daze
Wondering why you said I was special to you
Wondering why you said 'I love you'
You won the attention of another girl
I'll be the one who got away

It's Simple, Really

Love is not this ornate,
Complicated thing
Love is simple, really
Love is the golden rule
It's respect
And compassion
And honesty
No,
Love is not complicated
People are

You're My Type

Men.
Men and boys and dudes and bros.
You're a fun breed.
Witty. Passionate. Come in handy when lifting furniture.

You make me laugh, but I make myself laugh. In fact, I
might be funnier.
My friends make me laugh. Cats in Bread make me laugh.

You make me laugh.
You also make me shiver. My heart rate begins freestyling
around your every move. I revolve around your rigid steps.
Not quite a tango, but still a dance.

You're my type.
You check all my boxes. You also check into my box.
You fulfill the mirage of my abstract expectations.

You're my type.
You're athletic, intellectual, intimate, interesting.
Interesting.
You're Just My Type.
A man.

Women.

Women and girls and betches and ladies.

O, we're fun.

Mystical. Independent. Face it, women rock your world.

I make you laugh.

I make you wonder. I make you crave, crave for more.

More what?

I'm not sure. Let's find out.

I'm your type.

Charming. Stimulating. Sensual. I grab your attention, I try to hold on.

I'm your type.

I'm athletic, intellectual, intimate, interesting.

I'm Just Your Type.

I'm a woman.

Nothing Serious

Why would we take love seriously?
What a foolish desire, to surrender emotions
To lose sense of time for the sake of someone else

No, nothing serious
I don't take love like that
I'll dabble
Experience new people
But to pursue an adoration? No, That's too serious

Nothing serious
You're not the one
You're not my forever
You can't be my now

I'm not at that point of my life
To jeopardize it all, just because I met you
I was happy before I met you
Why let love get in the way

It's not the right time
I have so much going for me
I'm proud of who I am and who I will become
You will get in the way

I need my independence
I need my space
There's no forever
There's only now
Now I am happy
Why let love get in the way

PART II

You do not have to be in love to love
You do not have to be in love to be loved

Fingerpaint

She paints her nails
With glow-in-the-dark polish
So she can write her dreams at night

Powerful

Superman has his cape
But I have red lipstick
My power is turning heads
When I blow kisses
Superman has heat vision
Yet I can still see
All that melts before my eyes
When I spot what belongs to me

Beautiful Chaos

She stared at the coastline
In awe
Of the juxtaposition

>How could something so beautiful
>Be filled with such rage?
>We cross international waters but
>There is no certainty in the sea
>We can predict hurricanes
>But what about the riptide?

She stood by the shore and smiled
She had realized that
>Life imitates nature
That the erratic flow of the waves
Is what makes an ocean beautiful

An Ode To Ferris

Life moves fast but it's longer than you think

Single, Independent Woman

I do not wish for you to complete me
I am already whole
I do not want you to be my rock
I am already grounded
I don't need your hand to hold
But rather your ears to listen
To when I say that a woman like me
Will not be tamed
But rather is seeking the one
To take along for the ride

Voids

You ask me how I'm single
As if I know the answer
As if I've been doing it wrong the whole time
You ask how come a woman like me
Can't seem to find love
I told you that my end goal
Is not to seek The One
But to find a love within myself

Solitude

I challenge you
To be alone
To embrace your own silence
I ask that you
Put down your phone
Become your only reliance
We share and we post
We text and we ghost
Creating a fake alliance
Don't have your calling
Be building a following
So please
Just challenge yourself
To be alone
Stop liking the lives of others
Before working on your own

Haiku #2

The One is out there
Please do not get discouraged
I know that you do

You must be patient
For The One will also wait
Until they find you

Conservation

A canvas of skin
Stretches thick across flesh
Hugging bones that know brittle
Holding organs that remember pain
Now this skin
Reads stories from the scars that have healed
Written by wrinkles that have protected
Spoken through tired smiles that know truth
This skin is thick
And breathes like a canvas
But unlike art
It regenerates

Busy

I am single
But I am still worthy
I am alone
But I am not lonely
I am independent
But I still count on others
I am not in love
But rather busy
Loving myself

Muscle Memory

Do not be afraid
Of
Loving again

You still have the capacity

Just because you don't have a bike
Doesn't mean
You forgot how to ride

Reminder

Happiness exists when you allow it to

Instagood

My curated life
Is adored by the masses
You're seeing my day
Through rose colored glasses
You can like all you want
This photo of my face
I may be smiling
But I'm so out of place
I want you to know
There is more to me
Than all this you see
That what I don't post
Is what I deal with the most

Fake Followers

The lonely ones
Are often never alone
As they constantly seek
The attention they refuse
To give themselves

Some Brené Brown Ish

Vulnerability ain't so hard
When an open heart
Is all you can offer
Honesty is easy
When the truth is all you know
And all that you can speak

It's trusting others that's scary
Because the word of the world
Reads in different languages
When a billion voices scream at once
It's hard to tell who to listen to

So I speak my truth
In hopes that my vulnerability
Will lead the way
And the liars and cheats
Fall behind,
Muffled.
Silenced by self denial
Their distorted speech
Will be heard by their own kind
But this open heart
Attracts another
Because vulnerability isn't hard

When being vulnerable
Makes more sense
Than shutting down
And shying away
From all of the stories
That got us here in the first place

Dimensions

Time only exists in airports

She Must Be Italian

Mom called me fragile
Mistook my sensitivity
To call me fragile
Strips away my credibility

For the fragile must
Be handled with care
I was handed the wild card
I seek truth, but I choose dare

I may be broken
But I keep it together
And each time I fall
Is a walk to remember

I'd rather be broken
Than be labeled as frail
I'd rather come crashing
Break down, and prevail

Maturing

Not every decision will be good
But every lesson learned will be great

The Depressed Have It Easy

"You need to put yourself out there"
But here I am
Out there
Out of my house
I am here, "out there"
I put myself here
And do you know how hard that is?
The depressed have it easy
They stay locked in
Eyes locked on a screen
Depriving themselves from others
And feed their pain with vices
But today I went outside
And here I am
"Out there"

In The Now

This thing called mindfulness
What does it mean?
To be here in the now?
What about my dreams?
This thing called presence
It's about being calm
But how must I stay still
When yesterday's gone
Tomorrow is painfully lightyears away
So I worry about tomorrow
And miss all of today

Abundance

When the hardest part is breathing
Remember that there is no shortage of air
When your exhales are accompanied with tears
Remember that same air will dry up those tears
When breathing feels heavy
And words sound like cries
When waking up feels too daunting
Know that you have enough

Air

And all you have is time

Keep Ya Head Up

Times get tough
But skin is thick
Keep your chin up
And your heart open

And So I Published This Book

You are most capable
When you start

Sink or Swim

Open the tap
Filling up my soul
Grounding down
As water overflows

Tide rising
I float the brim
No need to breathe
When I know how to swim

I dive down
Diving deeper
I am the wanderer
I am the seeker

The farther I dive
The darker the water
I am unsure
But I am not bothered

For this is my path
This is my flow
I can't get lost
When there is everywhere to go

Meditation

Listen by breathing
Soften by staying still
Open up by shutting down
Let
Go
& begin to see with your eyes closed

Fun Facts

I used to mistake my insecurities for being insecure. And worse, I mistook other's online confidence for being confident. Turns out, it's understanding and embracing our insecurities that make us confident. It's noticing our weaknesses and admitting our wrongs that make us strong. Those people who have it all together? They don't. They put on a good production. *And they're probably exhausted.* It's people who laugh at themselves for their mistakes and comfort others when they see struggle that find true inner peace. And that shit isn't posted online. Because the people who show up in your life aren't commenting on your pics. They're at your door. Asking about your day. Indifferent to your insecurities because we're all unsure about something. It's being ok with those somethings and accepting each other's certain somethings that make us human. That make us a friend. That make us confident.

Freedom of Speech

There's an hierarchy of speech and somewhere near the bottom, we brag. We brag and we boast and we bitch about others. The more we bitch, the lower we go. Somewhere between ex-talk and eye rolls, we hit the bottom of the totem pole. We can talk about politics, art, food and wine; we can talk about travel which allows us to climb.

To keep climbing, we ask questions. We inquire. To get to the top, we talk dreams and inspire. Ideas and solutions keep us afloat so do not look down at that hate-talk we left so long ago.

Be careful what you say and be cautious of what you hear. There are those who talk light, and those who talk fear. Those who talk past tense, and that will keep them there.

Don't just talk, have a voice. Be grateful for this freedom as not everyone speaks because they don't have a choice.

Have Faith

Have faith. Trust yourself while removing arrogance. Set intentions and make mistakes. Reflect without ruminating and be patient in the process. Fear will arise. Embrace it. Because when you have faith, your fears cast your path towards bravery.

Love Your Body

Love your body
Love you hair, your skin, your smile
Love how your body changes with time
It reminds us that nothing is constant
Respect your body
Give it a hug
Sometimes the only human touch we crave is our own
Take notice of your body. Where are you strong? Where
is your fat?
Love your fat
Give it a pinch
It shows that you're alive
Love your fat. Love your freckles. Love your scars.
These physicalities fade
But you don't have to

So dance. Stretch. Run.
Move your body in ways you've never known before
Love your body
Because no one else can love it for you

The Game of Life

Who are you competing against? Your coworker and sister and best friend and the family down the street?

If so, What do you get for coming in first? Money? It's got to be money. But if the prize is money, are we aiming for greed?

No, the prize is ownership. Ownership of the house, the car, the health clubs and something that sheds with four legs.

No, the end goal of this game is love. Right? It's got to be love. To love someone and to have someone love you. To legalize your love in union and procreate little someone's to love you back.

Or maybe the prize is a combination of it all. Wealth in experiences and owning our actions. Falling in love with everything we do, displaying love towards others and most importantly, fostering love for ourselves.

Or perhaps there is no prize. Perhaps this isn't really a game. If life were a game then we would have winners and losers. Referees and players on the sidelines. No, this isn't a game. We aren't all in it to win it because *there is no prize*.

We are, however, all in it.

Smoke and Mirrors

When all your see in your reflection
Are red eyes and rejection
Know that same mirror
Is seeing you
A vision
The mirror is not blind
To your false perception

You are a vision

Take Care

Whether you are single, dating, in love, or married- no one can care about you as much as you do. All the warmth you receive from the people in your life may keep you comfortable, but you must create your own heat. Your own energy. The more you seek acceptance in others, the less time you spend understanding your own worth. So remove yourself from the world for once. Say no to plans. Take yourself on a date and make love to the only body you've been given, because it's incredible. There are so many people that care about you. But only you can take care of yourself.

Afterword

No one ever told me to become a writer, let alone a poet. I was raised in a sports-centric family in the safe suburbs of Kansas City and encouraged to take my athleticism to the collegiate level. I was also encouraged to pursue a business major as my father instilled, "If you want to make money, go into sales". I've learned now that it's 2019, and you can make money doing just about anything. Most importantly, I've learned you can earn a living *doing what you love.*

My first poems spurred from a few bad Bumble dates. Instead of texting the men who had rejected me, I realized it was much more acceptable to keep my thoughts to myself and express my feelings in a platform which was new to me. When the man I had been saying "I love you" to rejected me (and informed me that he was seeing someone else during our relationship), I wrote rapidly. Between the self-loathing and substance abuse, I mustered the strength to put this heartbreak into words. With each poem I released, the thought of him began to hurt less.

As I made progress from the breakup, my awareness with my job uncertainty began to arise. My therapist advised that instead of writing about the boy, to write about work. Eventually, the more that I wrote, the more I loathed driving to the office each morning. I began crying in my car, crying at my desk, and crying in the bathroom stalls, yearning to be anywhere else so I could write.

The day I quit my job I was determined to turn my poems into a book. For weeks, I showed up to the same seat at the library to write. I would set up my broken Macbook with it's external keyboard and mouse and wait until my fingertips started flowing. Under bright lights, tears poured down my cheeks as I wrote and rewrote poems about heartbreak and my eating disorder. Whenever I needed some comic relief, I wrote about work.

It's funny. As much as I see my writing as a gift, the fluidity of typing often comes with a cost. What is sometimes easy for me to put down in words is equally as painful to look up and read what I have created. But every time I wipe the tears from my eyes and digest my work, a sense of relief and joy emerges. This work is proof that I am a survivor.

I have read that if you're writing for somebody else or if you're writing to make money, don't write. Though this is not my intention for publishing this book, I dream that my poetry will heal the hearts of its readers the same way writing the poetry has helped me.

My words are my gift to you. We are all fighting for purpose; for love from others and love for ourselves. Let hope emerge. Know that you are worthy and *you are not alone.*

About the Author

Amidst writing this book, Jennifer juggled several part time jobs including dog sitting, liquor tastings, data entry and front desk greeter at a gym. She was enrolled in a 200 Hour Yoga Teacher Training as well as an ICF accredited life coaching program during the time of publication.

Jennifer hustles between transitions to remind herself and to others that what's easy may not be what's best, and what's difficult will always be worth it when done with intention. Jennifer now speaks her story as a voice of recovery to schools and events to promote body positivity, unconditional self-love, and connectedness.

Follow Jennifer:

Web: www.missjennifermartin.com
Facebook: www.facebook.com/jennifermartinofficial
Instagram: @miss.jennifer.martin
Twitter: @mjm_writes

CPSIA information can be obtained
at www.ICGtesting.com
Printed in the USA
FFHW022005180619
53088469-58702FF